APPLE AIRPODS PRO USER GUIDE

COMPREHENSIVE GUIDE AND ADVANCED TIPS FOR USING APPLE AIRPODS PRO

SCOTT DOWNING

Goodwater Publishing
279 Stoney Lane
Dallas, TX 75212
Texas
USA

CONTENTS

INTRODUCTION

Apple, on October 30, 2019, announced the release of Airpods Pro wireless earbuds. They include features of standard AirPods, such as a built-in microphone that filters out background noise, built-in accelerometers, and optical sensors that can detect presses on the stem and in-ear placement, and automatic pausing when they are taken out of the ears. Control by tapping is replaced by pressing a force sensor on the stems.

Just like Airpods 2, they are equipped with the Apple-designed H1 chip, which supports hands-free **Hey Siri** commands. Airpods Pro also features ten audio cores able to power real-time noise cancellation and deliver high-quality sound. Battery life is the same as the AirPods 2, lasting for up to five hours in standard mode. When Noise Cancellation is active, AirPods Pro offers up to four and a half hours of listening time and three and a half hours of talk time.

Apple's AirPods Pro is both sweat and water-resistant with an IPX4 rating. This means that they'll hold up to some light splashing and sweating, but submersion should be avoided. This also means that you will be able to take them to the gym and won't have to worry about getting caught in the rain storm, but you should not take them for a swim.

AirPods Pro is designed for comfort, and each earbud is shipped with three different sizes of silicone ear tips that conform to the contours of the individual ear. The best fit is chosen after an **Ear Tip Fit Test** is run to make sure you get the best audio experience. The result of the test will be able to tell whether the ear tip is the right size and has a good fit or should be adjusted for a better seal.

The included Wireless Charging Case can deliver more than 24 hours of listening time and over 18 hours of talk time. A USB-C to lightning cable is also included in the box for charging purposes.

AIRPODS PRO FEATURES

AirPods Pro feature several updates over the popular AirPods 2. So what's improved in the AirPods Pro compared to the previous AirPods?

System Requirements

The following Apple device models are fully supported by AirPods Pro depending on the version devices as long as they're signed in to iCloud with the same Apple ID account: If you have AirPods Pro, you need at least one of these:

- iPhone and iPod touch with iOS 13.2 or later
- iPad with iPadOS 13.2 or later
- Apple Watch with watchOS 6.1 or later
- Apple TV with tvOS 13.2 or later
- Mac with macOS 10.15.1 or later

Design

Each of the AirPods Pro earbuds measures and weighs:

- Height: 30.9mm (1.22 inches)

- Width: 21.8 mm (0.86 inch)

- Depth: 24.0mm (0.94 inch)

- Weight: 5.4 grams

While the wireless charging case measures and weighs:

- Height: 45.2 mm (1.78 inches)

- Width: 60.6 mm (2.39 inches)

- Depth: 21.7 mm (0.85 inch)

- Weight: 45.6 grams

From the dimensions above, it's clear that the carry case, which doubles as the charging case, is now shorter in height, but wider in design. It's still very much just as pocketable as before and comes in the same gloss white.

For the AirPods Pro earbuds, the weight is considerably heavier, and the stem is shorter than the previous AirPods. They also lack tap controls like the previous AirPods; instead, you force touch (press) the stem to play/pause, move forward, or go back to a song.

The AirPods Pro earbuds slot into the case in a similar way to the earlier models of AirPods and instantly start charging. Charging can be done via a Lightning cable or by putting the case on a wireless Qi-compatible charging pad.

Finding your fit

One of the noticeable differences in the AirPods Pro is the inclusion of silicone tips (form-fitting rubber tips that hold the AirPods Pro in your ear solidly) to improve the fit. The AirPods Pro comes with three differently-sized tips – there is a small, medium, and large options included. The software in iOS 13.2 lets your iPhone run an ear tip fit test, which tells you which tips are the best fit for your ears. Unlike the earlier versions of AirPods, the Pro requires a subsequent step, which involves you running an **Ear Tip Fit Test**.

The test process involves playing some music which takes about five seconds. It's during this time that it will determine whether you've got a good fit and if not, recommend you change the silicone tip to another size. As the silicone tips feel a little tight in the ear, the AirPods Pro is equipped with an air vents technology known as Vent System. It's designed to equalize pressure to minimize discomfort familiar with other in-ear designs.

Active Noise Cancelation and Transparency Mode

AirPods Pro has three noise-control modes: **Active Noise Cancellation**, **Transparency Mode**, and **Off**. You can switch between them, depending on how much of your surroundings you want to hear.

The AirPods Pro's Active Noise Cancellation (ANC) feature uses two in-built microphones (one outward-facing to detect environmental noise and one inward-facing towards the ear) to check the ambient noise around you over 200 times per second and react accordingly by removing background noise.

Transparency mode offers users the option to listen to music while still hearing what's going on around them, for situations like biking in traffic or listening to an important train message. Transparency mode takes advantage of the vent system in the AirPods Pro to leave just the right amount of noise cancellation.

Swapping between Active Noise Cancellation and Transparency mode can be done using a new force sensor system that Apple has added to the stem of the AirPods Pro. This force sensor can also be used to play, pause, or skip tracks and answer and hang up phone calls. The mode can also be controlled through the Control Center or by asking Siri on iPhone and iPad; or Apple Watch by tapping the AirPlay icon while music is playing.

Battery life

Battery life is the same as the AirPods 2, lasting for up to five hours in standard mode. When Noise Cancellation is active, AirPods Pro offers up to four and a half hours of listening time and three and a half hours of talk time with a single charge. The AirPods Pro with the wireless charging case offers more than 24 hours of listening time and more than 18 hours of talk time. Five minutes in the case provides around one hour of listening time or around one hour of talk time.

Sound Quality

AirPods Pro is designed to deliver superior sound quality with Adaptive EQ, a feature that automatically tunes the low and mid frequencies of the music to the shape of an individual's ear.

AIRPODS PRO VERSUS AIRPODS 2 COMPARISON

	AirPods Pro	AirPods 2
Dimensions (inches)	1.22 x 0.86 x 0.94	1.59 x 0.65 x 0.71
Weight (grams)	5.4	4.0
Case Dimensions (inches)	1.78 x 2.39 x 0.85	2.11 x 1.74 x 0.84
Case Weight (grams)	45.6	40.0
Battery Life (AirPods)	4.5 Hours with ANC, 5 Hours with ANC off	5 Hours
Battery Life (with Case)	More than 24 Hours	More than 24 Hours
Connectivity	Bluetooth 5.0	Bluetooth 5.0
Microphones	Dual Beam forming, Single Inward-Facing	Dual Beam forming
Sensors	Dual Optical Sensors, Motion-	Dual Optical Sensors, Motion-

	Detecting Accelerometer, Speech-Detecting Accelerometer, Force Sensor	Detecting Accelerometer, Speech-Detecting Accelerometer
Sweat and Water Resistance	IPX4	No
Active Noise Cancellation	Yes	No

CONNECT AND USE YOUR AIRPODS PRO

Unboxing the AirPods Pro

In the box, Apple includes the following:

- AirPods Pro

- Wireless Charging Case

- Silicone ear tips (three sizes)

- Lightning to USB-C Cable

Setting up Airpods Pro

Setting up AirPods Pro for the first time is extremely simple and quick with any Bluetooth compatible device but more comfortable to use your iPhone or iPad to do so. Your iCloud account will be used to sync pairing information on other Apple devices without the need for any additional pairing. This auto-pairing feature works on all compatible iPhone, iPad, iPod, Apple Watch, Apple TV, and Mac listed in the earlier section of this book.

Pairing AirPods Pro with Your iPhone or iPad

Pairing AirPods Pro with the iPhone or iPad is easy to set up with an Apple device. After unboxing your AirPods Pro, all you need to do is unlock your iPhone or iPad, pop open the top of the AirPods Pro wireless charging case, hold it near your device, and wait for a popup on your iPhone or iPad's display. You'll see an animated graphic of the case opening; from there, you tap the connect button and the AirPods Pro pairs like magic.

AirPods Pro is designed to connect to your iPhone or iPad whenever you open the case lid, so all you need to do to listen to music is take them out of the case and put them in your ears. There could be a situation whereby you will need to pair your iPhone with your AirPods Pro manually. In such a case, follow the following steps to set it up manually:

1. Unbox and remove the AirPods from the packaging
2. Leave the AirPods Pro in charging case and close the lid
3. Power on your iPhone or iPad, unlock it, and go to the Home screen
4. Open up the case with your AirPods Pro inside
5. Hold the AirPods Pro case with open lid next to your iPhone or iPad

6. Your iOS device will recognize the AirPods Pro and you'll see an animated graphic of the case opening prompting you to connect your AirPods Pro

7. Tap **Connect** to pair your AirPods Pro to your iPhone

8. After pairing, about three different screens walk you through how to use some of your new AirPods Pro's features such as noise cancellation and Force Sensor's press-and-hold Transparency Mode activation.

9. The setup process will further ask if you want Siri to read incoming messages through the AirPods Pro without having to unlock your iPhone. To enable this feature, select the **Announce Messages With Siri** button. If not, tap the **Not Now** link.

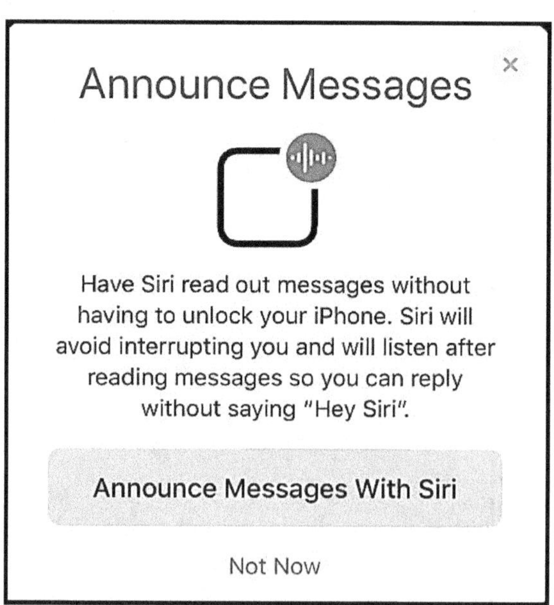

10. A popup will display the battery life for both the AirPods Pro and the case. Tap **Done** to close the popup.

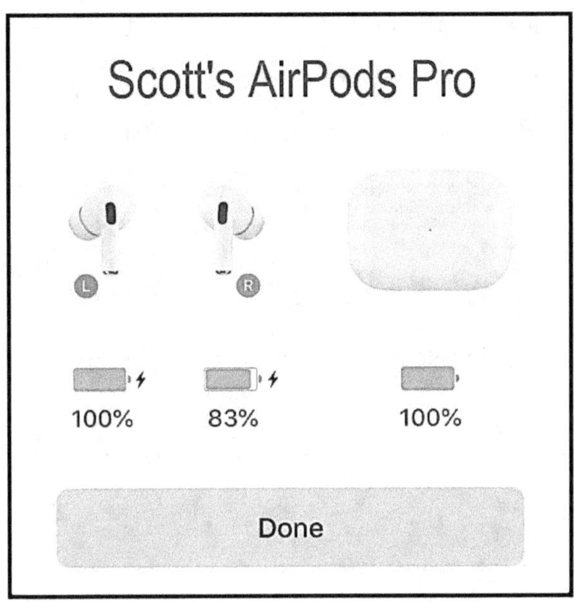

That's all there is to it. Once this setup process has been completed, your AirPods Pro will re-pair to your iOS device whenever you open up the case lid. This re-pairing process takes just a few seconds, so your AirPods Pro is fundamentally ready to go whenever you pull them out.

If you have **iCloud** configured on your iPhone, the AirPods Pro's pairing will be shared with your other Apple devices. In other words, if you're signed in to iCloud, your AirPods are set up automatically with any of your supported devices that are signed in to iCloud with the same Apple ID.

Pairing AirPods Pro with Your Mac

If you've set up AirPods Pro with your iPhone and your Mac is signed in to iCloud with the same Apple ID, then your AirPods Pro should be ready to use with your Mac. Ideally, all you need to do is put your AirPods Pro in your ears, click the **Bluetooth** icon in your Mac's menu bar, select your AirPods Pro from the dropdown list, and click **Connect**.

However, if it wasn't automatic or if you don't see your AirPods Pro in the **Bluetooth** menu, you can pair them manually with your Mac in the following way:

1. On your Mac, select **System Preferences** from the Apple menu bar
2. Click the **Bluetooth** icon
3. Make sure the Bluetooth is turned on
4. With your AirPods Pro in their charging case, open the lid
5. Press and hold the button on the back of the charging case until the status light between the AirPods Pro flashes white
6. You should then see the name of the AirPods Pro appear in the **Bluetooth Devices** list of Mac
7. Select your AirPods Pro and click **Connect**

Next time you want to use your AirPods Pro with your Mac, place them in your ears, and they should automatically pair. If they don't (if they pair with your nearby iPhone instead, for example) simply click the Bluetooth icon in your Mac's menu bar, select your AirPods Pro in the dropdown list, and click **Connect**.

Pairing AirPods Pro with Your Apple Watch

Once you've paired a new set of AirPods Pro with an iPhone running iOS 13.2 or later, they should automatically pair with your Apple Watch as long as your watch's software is up to date. AirPods Pro requires watchOS 6.1 or later. Once your Apple Watch firmware is up to date, your connected AirPods Pro will automatically switch their connection between iPhone and Apple Watch, depending on which one is playing audio.

However, you can also manually connect your AirPods Pro to your Apple Watch whenever you like. Here's how it's done.

1. Put your AirPods Pro in the charging case

2. Open the lid, but don't remove AirPods Pro yet

3. Press and hold the circular setup button on the back near the bottom of the charging case until the status light between your AirPods Pro at the top of the case starts rhythmically blinking white.

4. On your Apple Watch, swipe up from the bottom of the screen to bring up the **Control Center**. (If you're in an app, touch and hold the bottom edge of the screen, then drag up the Control Center pane with your finger.)

5. Tap the **AirPlay** icon (the small triangle with concentric circles on top).

6. Select the name of your AirPods Pro and tap **Connect**.

Alternatively, you can also open up the **Settings** on the Apple Watch, go to the **Bluetooth** section, and choose **AirPods Pro** from the list of available devices. Tap to connect.

Pairing AirPods Pro with Your Apple TV

Apple TV does not support AirPods Pro pairing via iCloud, so you must manually pair them to the device. This makes it easy to listen to movies, TV shows, and other media without disturbing the people around you. The process of pairing AirPods Pro manually with Apple TV is the same as that for connecting standard Bluetooth headphones. Note that to connect successfully, AirPods Pro requires your Apple TV to be running tvOS 13.2 (or later) to be installed.

1. Put your AirPods Pro in the charging case.
2. If you aren't already wearing your AirPods Pro, make sure to at least flip the lid open on the charging case before continuing.
3. Press and hold the circular button on the back of the AirPods Pro charging case until the light inside the case between the AirPods Pro starts flashing white. This means that AirPods Pro earbuds are in Bluetooth discovery mode.
4. On your Apple TV, go to **Settings**.
5. Navigate to **Remotes and Devices** and select **Bluetooth**.
6. Select your AirPods Pro when they appear in the **Other Devices** list.

7. Click **Connect Device** to initiate the pairing process. Once complete, your AirPods will be connected to your Apple TV and ready to use.

Pairing AirPods Pro with Your non-Apple devices

To pair your AirPods Pro manually with a Windows PC, Android smartphone or tablet or other non-Apple device with Bluetooth support, follow the steps below.

1. Put your AirPods Pro in the charging case.

2. Open the lid, but don't remove AirPods Pro yet

3. Press and hold the circular setup button on the back near the bottom of the charging case until the status light between your AirPods Pro at the top of the case starts rhythmically blinking white.

4. On your host non-Apple device, engage in the Bluetooth pairing process like you normally would and follow any on-screen prompts to finish setting up your AirPods Pro.

UNPAIRING AIRPODS PRO

It's worth noting that unpairing AirPods Pro from your iPhone, Apple Watch or Mac automatically removes them from all your other iPhone, iPad, Mac and Apple Watch devices that are signed in to the same iCloud account. It may take a few seconds for AirPodsPro to disconnect from all your iCloud devices. They remain paired with other devices that don't support iCloud pairing (i.e. Apple TVs, Windows PCs and Android smartphones and tablets) until manually unpaired through their respective Bluetooth settings menu.

Unpairing AirPods Pro from iPhone or iPad

1. Go to **Settings** on your iPhone
2. Select **Bluetooth**
3. Tap the **circled i** next to your AirPods Pro in the **Devices** list.
4. A warning message appears saying that removing AirPods Pro from this device will automatically remove them from all your other iCloud-signed devices.
5. Tap **Forget This Device**.
6. Confirm the action by tapping **Forget This Device** in the popup menu.

Unpairing AirPods Pro from Mac

1. On your Mac, click the **Apple** icon in the menu bar and select **System Preferences**

2. Click the **Bluetooth** icon in the Preference pane

3. Right-click (or Ctrl+click) your AirPods Pro in the **Devices** list

4. Click **Remove** in the contextual menu that appears

5. Click **Remove** again to confirm the action

Unpairing AirPods Pro from Apple Watch

1. On your Apple Watch, go to **Settings**

2. Click on **Bluetooth**

3. Tap the **circled i** next to your AirPods Pro in the list

4. Tap **Forget Device**

Unpairing AirPods Pro from Apple TV

1. On your Apple TV, go to **Settings**

2. Select **Remotes and Devices** and click on **Bluetooth**

3. Select your AirPods Pro in the **Devices** list

4. A dialog pops up warning you that **Your Apple TV is connected to this device**

5. Select **Forget Device** to disconnect the AirPods Pro earbuds

Unpairing AirPods Pro from non-Apple devices

AirPods Pro acts like ordinary Bluetooth earphones when used with non-Apple hardware, meaning that they can be unpaired as quickly as say Bluetooth keyboard or mouse.

CHARGING YOUR AIRPODS PRO

New Apple AirPods Pro usually come fully charged out of the box, but at some point, during use, you'll hear a tone when your AirPods Pro earbuds' batteries are low and another tone just before they run out. At this point, it's time to charge the earbuds by simply putting them in the case and close the lid. AirPods Pro earbuds shut down and charge whenever they're in the case, allowing you to charge on the go. But at some point, the charging case will also become depleted, and then it will need charging too. Charging Case can be charged with a Qi-certified charger.

Place the case on the charger with the status light facing up and with the lid closed, to start charging it. The case's light will light up when it's first placed on the charger, letting you know it's charging. However, it will eventually time out and turn off. Tap the case when it is on the charging mat to check the charge status.

To charge your case via a wired connection, plug the Lightning cable that came with your AirPods Pro into the Lightning connector on your case. You can use a Lightning to USB-C or USB cable. Then plug the other end of the cable into a USB charger or port. You can charge your case with or without your AirPods Pro inside. Charging is fastest when you use an iPhone or iPad USB charger or plug into your Mac.

Deciphering charging case status light states

The status light is in front of the case for the wireless charging case. If your AirPods Pro is in your case and the lid is open, then the LED light indicates the charge status of your AirPods Pro. When your AirPods Pro isn't in your case, the light shows the charge status of your charging case.

Here's how to interpret the status light:

- Green—Fully charged.

- Orange—Not fully charged.

- Amber—Less than one full charge remains.

- Flashing white—AirPods Pro is ready to pair with your devices or is in pairing mode.

- Flashing Amber—You will likely need to set up your AirPods Pro again before using them.

CHECKING YOUR AIRPODS BATTERY LIFE

There are a few easy ways to check how much battery life you have on each AirPod Pro and the charging case.

Checking AirPods Pro battery life with charging case

One of the fastest ways to check how much battery you have left on your AirPods Pro or the charging case, place the AirPods Pro into the charging case and keep the lid open next to your iPhone. A pop-up should appear that shows how much battery you have left on your AirPod Pro and the charging case.

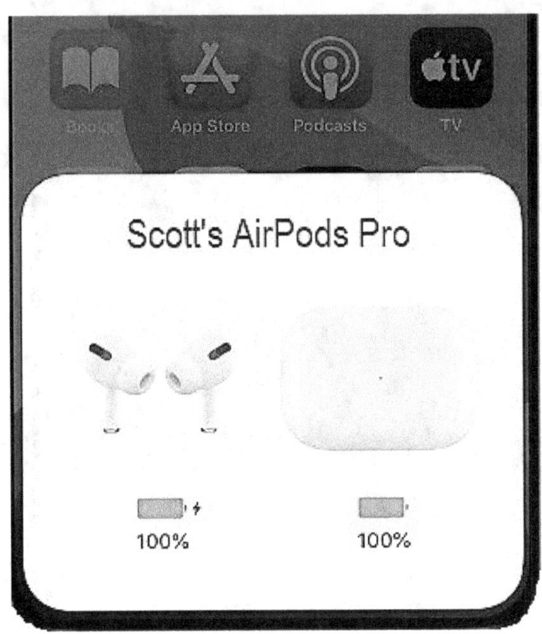

Checking AirPods Pro battery life with Batteries widget

Another way to check is to use the Batteries widget to check the current battery level in any Bluetooth audio accessory connected to your iOS device, including AirPods Pro earbuds and the charging case. Simply go to the Notification Center on your iPhone by pulling down from the screen top, then swipe right to the widgets screen, and select the Batteries widget. Now you'll see the battery percentage of your AirPods Pro and the charging case on the Widget page, as well as the battery percentage of your iPhone and any other connected device (Apple Watch, etc.). The charge for your case appears only when at least one AirPod is in the case.

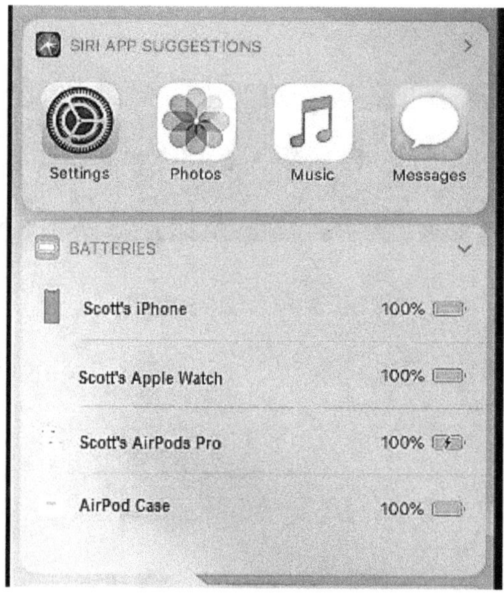

If the Batteries widget is not already enabled, you can add it first to your active widgets.

1.	On your **Home** page, swipe to the right right to access your widget page.

2.	Scroll down and click **Edit.**

3.   Find the battery widget and click the **green +** icon to enable the widget.

4.   Click **Done** to save.

Checking AirPods Pro battery life on Mac

All you will need to do is click the Bluetooth symbol in the menu bar of your Mac. Using your cursor, highlight the AirPods, Pro, and then there will be a sub-menu that shows you all information. This sub-menu will give you the ability to disconnect, along with showing the left and right AirPods Pro battery. You can even see the remaining battery of the AirPods Pro case if you need to know whether it's time for a charge.

Checking AirPods battery life by asking Siri

Another way to check the battery life of AirPods Pro on your iPhone is with the help of Siri. Just say out loud **Hey Siri** and ask **How's the battery on my AirPods Pro today?** Siri responds with the amount of battery remaining in your AirPods Pro.

Checking AirPods Pro battery life via Apple Watch

If you're an Apple Watch wearer, you can still check your AirPods Pro battery life by swiping up from your watch face to reveal the Control Center. Tap the battery percentage indicator in Control Center to see the AirPods Pro battery life.

LISTENING WITH YOUR AIRPODS PRO

Each AirPod Pro earbuds has either **L** or **R** printed on it to denote their orientation. Place left AirPod Pro in your left ear and right AirPod Pro in your right ear. The optical sensor inside each AirPod Pro enables it to play sound as soon as it's in your ear. When you take your AirPods Pro out of the case, they're on and ready to use. When you put them in your ears, your AirPods Pro earbuds automatically play the audio from your device. If you take any of the earbuds out, audio pauses. In other words, whatever song, podcasts, audiobook, or other audio content was playing gets paused until you put it back in your ear. Take them both out, and audio stops. If you're listening with one AirPods Pro earbud and you take it out, the earbud pauses. If you put it back in your ear within 15 seconds, play resumes automatically.

Making and Receiving Calls with AirPods Pro

To make a hands-free call while wearing AirPods Pro earbuds, you simply say **Hey Siri** to activate **Siri** and simply ask her to call one of your contacts. For instance, you can just say **Call John's mobile** or **Call dad's mobile**.

To answer a call with AirPods Pro, press the **Force Sensor** on the stem of either **Left** or **Right** AirPod to answer it. During the call, you can press the **Force Sensor** again to hang up or switch to another incoming call.

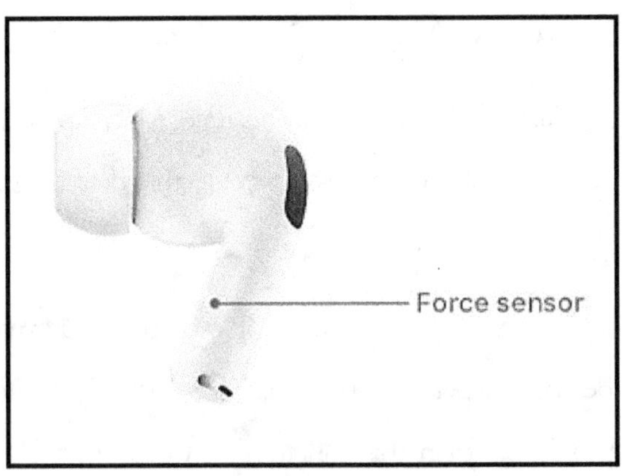

Force Sensor Controls

The following controls are available by pressing the Force Sensor:

- Press once (single press) to play, pause, or answer a phone call

- Press twice (double press) to skip forward

- Press three times (triple press) to skip back

- Press and hold (long press) to switch between Active Noise Cancellation and Transparency mode

SWITCHING AUDIO OUTPUT TO AIRPODS PRO

Once you pair your AirPods Pro to an iPhone, iPad, Mac, Apple Watch, or Apple TV, the wireless earbuds will attempt to connect to that device again the next time you use them.

Some Bluetooth headphones are capable of switching automatically between multiple paired devices, depending on which one is playing audio. However, AirPods Pro will only perform this function between your iPhone and Apple Watch. In all other cases, AirPods Pro will simply attempt to link up to the last-connected device. If you want your AirPods Pro to connect to another Apple device they've paired up with in the past, you have to do it manually.

Before you begin, make sure you've paired your AirPods Pro to at least one of the devices you want to switch between. AirPods Pro synchronizes pairing information through your iCloud account, enabling them to be connected to your other Apple devices without the need for any additional pairing.

If you aren't already wearing your AirPods Pro, make sure to at least flip the lid open on the charging case before continuing.

Switching iOS Device Audio Output to AirPods Pro

The AirPods Pro should start playing audio from your iOS devices automatically. However, if for some reason you need to change your audio output manually, follow these steps.

- Go to **Control Center**
- Tap the small **AirPlay** icon in the upper right corner of the playback controls panel

- Select your AirPods Pro from the **Devices** list.

Switching Apple Watch Audio Output to AirPods Pro

As mentioned above, AirPods Pro connected to your iPhone will automatically switch to your Apple Watch if you play audio directly from the AppleWatch. However, you can also manually connect to Apple Watch at any time using the following method.

- On your Apple Watch, swipe up from the bottom of the screen to bring up the **Control Center**.
- Tap the **AirPlay** icon (the small triangle with concentric circles on top).
- Select your AirPods from the list of devices.

Switching Mac Audio Output to AirPods Pro

To connect your Mac audio output to your AirPods Pro, click the **Volume** icon or the **Bluetooth** icon in your Mac's menu bar, select your AirPods Pro in the dropdown list, and click **Connect**.

Note: If you don't see the Volume or Bluetooth icon in your Mac's menu bar, go to **System Preferences** and click the **Sound** or **Bluetooth** pane, then tick the checkbox next to **Show volume in menu bar** or **Show Bluetooth in menu bar**.

Switching Apple TV Audio Output to AirPods Pro

To connect your Apple TV audio output to AirPods Pro, navigate to the Apple TV **Home** screen, hold the **Play/Pause** button on your Apple TV Remote, and then select your AirPods Pro from the panel list that appears.

ADVANCED TIPS AND CUSTOMIZATION OF AIRPODS PRO

There are a lot of features that make the new wireless earbuds a solid choice for Apple fans. To help you make the most of your AirPods Pro, here are some tips to help you master your new AirPods Pro straight out of the box.

How to Change the Name of Your AirPods Pro

Once you've successfully paired your new AirPods Pro to an iPhone or iPad, Apple will give your AirPods Pro the default name **[Your Name]'s AirPods Pro**, for instance, **Scott's AirPods Pro**. If you want, you can change this name by following the simple steps below.

1. Open your iPhone's **Settings** menu.
2. Tap **Bluetooth.**
3. Look for your AirPods Pro on the list of devices. Note that they must be connected and within range.
4. Tap the **circled i** next to your AirPods Pro.
5. At the next screen, tap **Name** and then input a new name for your AirPods Pro using the onscreen virtual keyboard.

How to Change the Name of AirPods Pro on Mac

You can also rename your AirPods Pro on your Mac. Simply follow these steps to do so.

1. On your Mac, launch **System Preferences.**
2. Click the **Bluetooth** pane.

3. With your AirPods Pro connected to your Mac, right-click them in the **Devices** list and then select **Rename** in the pop-up menu

4. Type in a new name for your AirPods Pro.

5. Click the **Rename** button to confirm.

How to Adjust Force Sensor Duration

If you're having difficulty engaging the AirPods' Force sensor by squeezing it between your fingers, try adjusting the duration to see if it makes it any easier. Follow these steps to adjust it.

1. Go to **Settings** on your iPhone or iPad.

2. Tap **Accessibility** and select **AirPods**.

3. Under **Press and Hold** Duration, select **Default, Short** or **Shorter**.

How to Change AirPods Pro Force Sensor Press Speed

The Force Sensor controls on AirPods Pro allow you to press once to play, pause or answer a phone call, press twice to skip forward, and press three times to skip backward. Like the press-and-hold gesture, if you're having trouble engaging these functions, then you can adjust the press speed to make it slower. Follow these steps to change it.

1. Go to **Settings** on your iPhone or iPad.

2. Tap **Accessibility** and select **AirPods**.

3. Under **Press Speed**, select **Default, Slow** or **Slowest**.

How to Customize the Force Sensor Gesture Functions on AirPods Pro

Apple's AirPods Pro wireless earbuds feature a new, innovative force sensor on each stem that responds to gestures which you can use to play/pause and skip tracks, answer and hang up phone calls, and switch between Active Noise Cancellation and Transparency modes. By default, you can press and hold either AirPod Pro stem to cycle between the Noise Cancellation and Transparency Modes (you'll hear a tone when switching between the two functions). You can also customize the press-and-hold gestures. Here's how it works.

1. Allow your AirPods to connect to your iPhone or iPad in the usual way, by opening the case next to your device and inserting the buds in your ears.

2. Go to **Settings** on your iPhone.

3. Tap **Bluetooth.**

4. Under **My Devices**, tap the **circled i** next to AirPods Pro in the list.

5. Under **Press and Hold AirPods**, tap **Left** or **Right**, depending on which AirPods Pro earbud you want to be customized.

6. To activate Siri with a press-and-hold gesture, tap **Siri.**

7. To change the Noise Control features that are activated via a press-and-hold gesture, tap **Noise Control** so that it's ticked, then tap the functions below that you want to assign to it. The options are **Noise Cancellation, Transparency**, and **Off** (which disables noise cancellation and transparency mode).

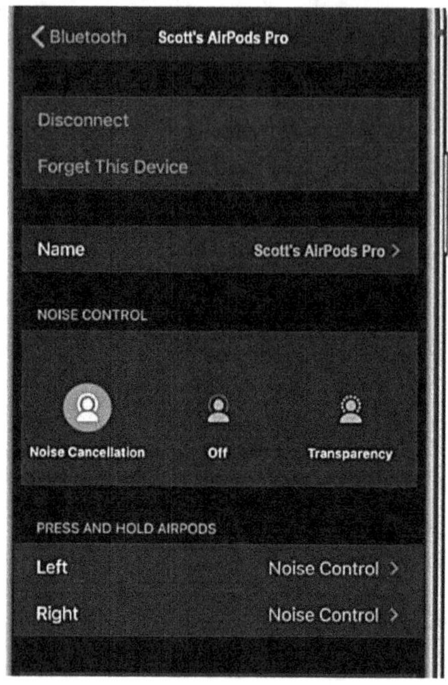 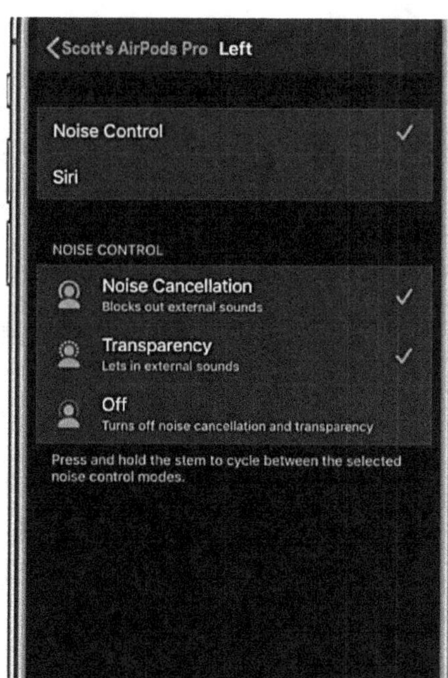

Note that you can assign more than one noise control feature to the press-and-hold gesture on either earbud – pressing and holding the stem will cycle between the selected modes.

How to Enable Active Noise Cancellation (ANC)

The AirPods Pro Active Noise Cancellation (ANC) is the standout feature of the new wireless earbuds. With ANC, an outward-facing microphone detects external sounds, which your AirPods Pro then counter with anti-noise, canceling the external sounds before you hear them. An inward-facing microphone listens inside your ear for unwanted internal sounds, which your AirPods Pro also counter with anti-noise. You can enable ANC right from your AirPods Pro, or you can use your iPhone, iPad, Apple Watch, or Mac.

From AirPods Pro:

You can enable ANC from the AirPods Pro by long-pressing Force Sensor on one of the stems of your AirPods Pro earbuds until you hear a ding sound effect (you'll feel/hear a soft click as well).

From iPhone or iPad:

To enable ANC from the iPhone or iPad, follow these steps:

Method 1: Opening Control Center

1. Open **Control Center** on your iPhone by swiping down from the top-right of the screen.
2. Long press on the volume slider (make sure your AirPods Pro earbuds are connected).
3. At the bottom of the screen, you'll have three options: Noise cancellation, Transparency and Off. Tap **Noise Cancelation** button in the slider.

Method 2: Opening Bluetooth Settings

You can enable ANC in Settings on your iPhone or iPad:

1. Go to **Settings** and select **Bluetooth.**
2. Tap **circled i** next to your AirPods Pro in the list of devices.
3. Tap **Noise Cancelation** button which is the same as ANC.

From Apple Watch:

Noise Cancellation can be enabled or disabled from Apple Watch and here's how it's being done.

1. While listening to audio through your watch, tap the **AirPlay** icon.

2. Tap **Noise Cancellation.**

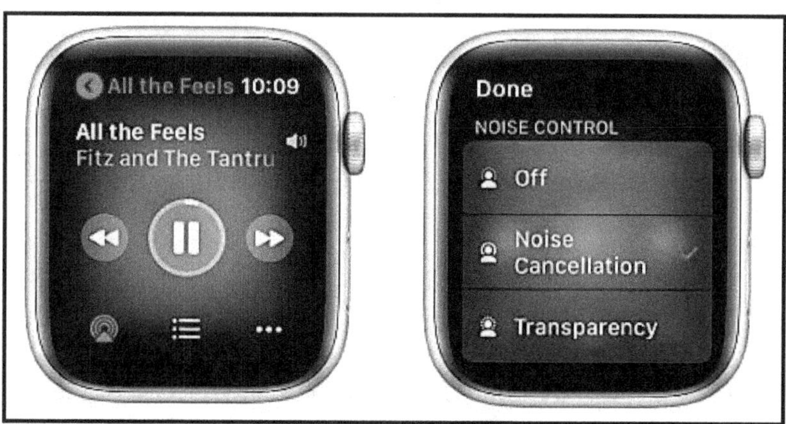

From Mac:

Enabling or disabling ANC from Mac is easy and here's how it's being done.

1. With your AirPods Pro connected to your Mac, click the **Volume control** in the menu bar on your Mac.

2. Choose your AirPods Pro, and then tap to tick **Noise Cancellation** which is the same as ANC.

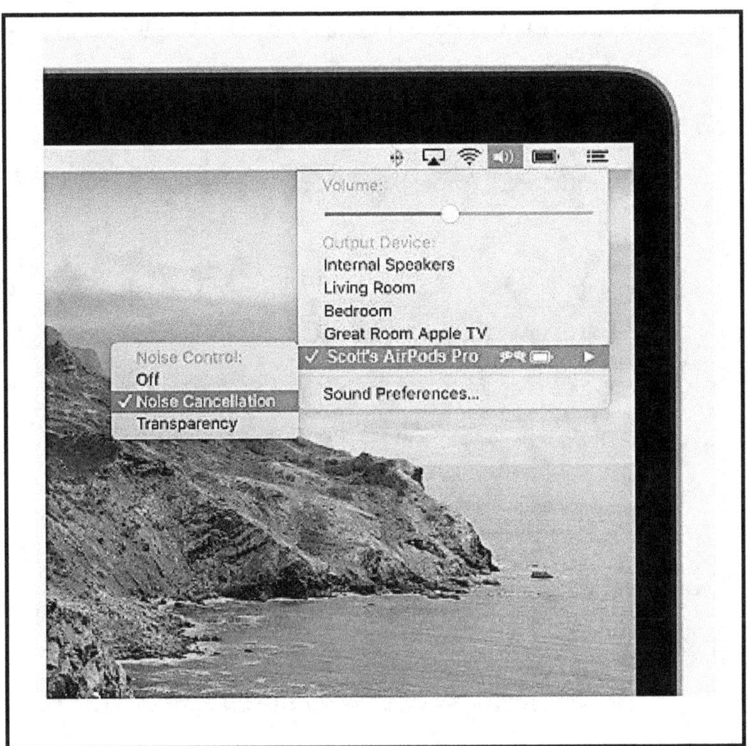

How to Enable Active Noise Cancellation on One AirPod

You can use ANC when using only one AirPod Pro, which is useful if you like to take calls using just the one earbud. Follow these steps to enable it.

1. Go to **Settings** on your iPhone or iPad.

2. Tap **Accessibility** and select **AirPods**.

3. Tap the toggle next to **Noise Cancellation on One AirPod** to enable it.

How to Use Transparency Mode

AirPods Pro also has another mode in addition to ANC called Transparency Mode. Transparency Mode allows you to temporarily let outside noise in through your AirPods Pro even when ANC is engaged. This is helpful in situations when you need to hear an announcement, such as on the train or a busy street while out on the run. You can also enable Transparency Mode from your AirPods Pro, or you can use your iPhone, iPad, Apple Watch, or Mac to enable it.

From AirPods Pro:

You can enable Transparency Mode from the AirPods Pro by long pressing Force Sensor on one of the stems of your AirPods Pro earbuds until you hear a ding sound effect (you'll feel/hear a soft click as well).

From iPhone or iPad:

To enable Transparency Mode from the iPhone or iPad, follow these steps:

Method 1: Opening Control Center

4. Open **Control Center** on your iPhone by swiping down from the top-right of the screen.

5. Long press on the volume slider (make sure your AirPods Pro earbuds are connected).

6. At the bottom of the screen, you'll have three options: Noise cancellation, Transparency and Off. Tap **Transparency Mode** button in the slider.

Method 2: Opening Bluetooth Settings

You can also Transparency Mode in Settings on your iPhone or iPad:

4. Go to **Settings** and select **Bluetooth**.

5. Tap **circled i** next to your AirPods Pro in the list of devices.

6. Tap **Transparency Mode** button.

From Apple Watch:

Transparency Mode can also be enabled or disabled from Apple Watch and here's how it's being done.

3. While listening to audio through your watch, tap the **AirPlay** icon.
4. Tap **Transparency Mode**.

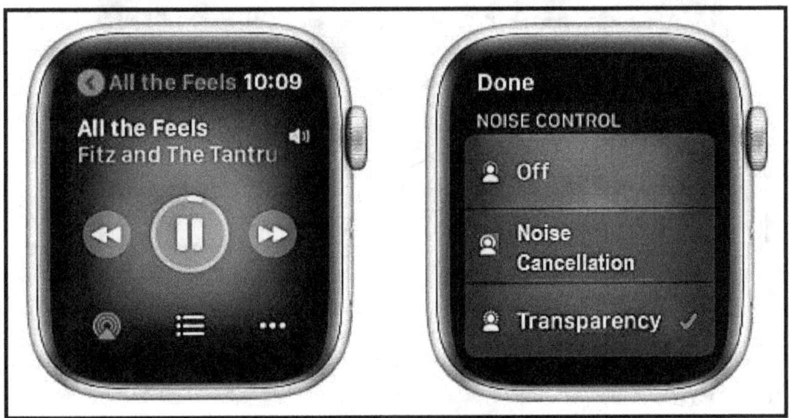

From Mac:

Enabling or disabling ANC from Mac is easy and here's how it's being done.

3. With your AirPods Pro connected to your Mac, click the **Volume control** in the menu bar on your Mac.
4. Choose your AirPods Pro, and then tap to tick **Noise Cancellation** which is the same as ANC.

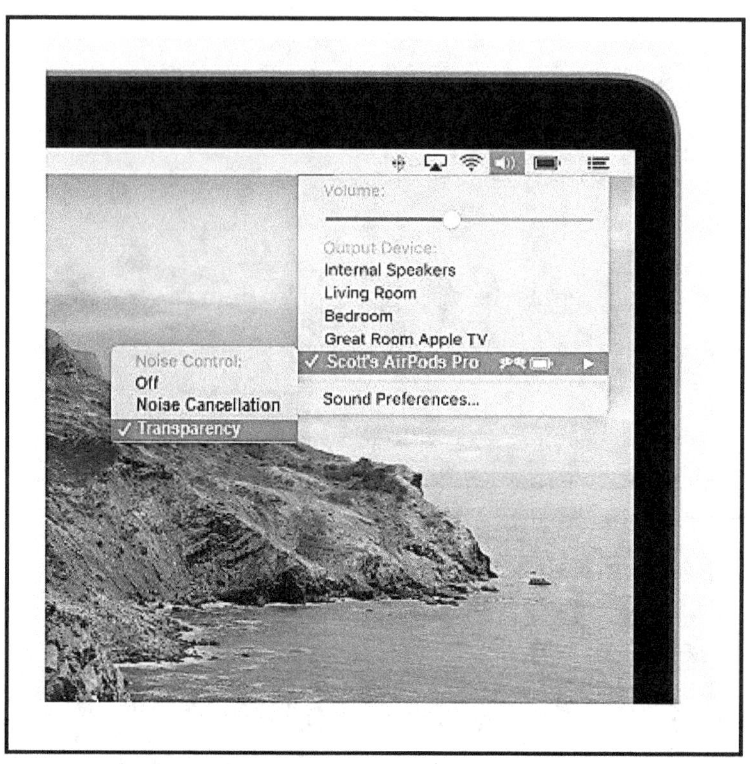

How to Enable or Disable Automatic Ear Detection on Your AirPods Pro

AirPods Pro comes with a feature called Automatic Ear Detection that allows the audio routed from a connected device to seamlessly switch to the AirPods Pro earbuds the moment you put them in your ears. This means the AirPods Pro can automatically pause the audio track when you remove them and resume playback when you put them back in again, ensuring you won't miss a thing.

This feature is enabled by default, but you can manually disable or enable it by following the simple steps below.

1.   Open your iPhone's or iPad's **Settings** menu

2.	Tap **Bluetooth**

3.	Under the **My Devices** list, tap the **circled i** next to your connected AirPods Pro.

4.	Toggle **On** or **Off** the switch next to **Automatic Ear Detection.**

How to run the AirPods Pro Ear Tip Fit Test

AirPods Pro comes with three different sets of ear tips for a customizable fit, and they also have a neat fit-test feature that uses the internal microphones to analyze whether you've picked the right ear tips. In this test, a song is played back for around five seconds to help you find out the best ear tip size. The good thing about this test is that it will determine the right ear tip size for both ears individually. To run this test, do the following:

1.	With your AirPods Pro earbuds in your ears, go to **Settings** on your iPhone.

2.	Select Bluetooth and tap **circled i** next to your AirPods Pro listed in the Bluetooth devices.

3.	Tap **Ear Tip Fit Test.**

4.	Choose **Continue** to run the test

5.	Tap the **Play** button.

6. After the sound plays, the screen will tell you if your chosen ear tips are a good fit or if you should try another one.

7. Tap **Done** in the top right corner when finished.

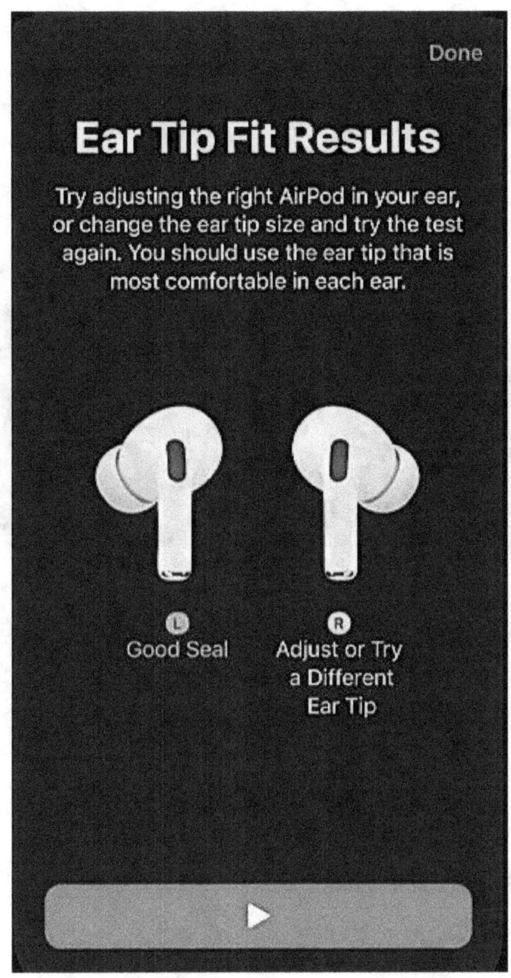

How to Change AirPods Pro Ear Tips

1. Look for the small square box in the bottom of the larger AirPods Pro box.

2. Remove the ear tips you'd like to use (give a firm pull, as they're securely attached to the packaging).

3. Give another firm pull on the medium-sized ear tips that come installed on AirPods Pro to remove them.

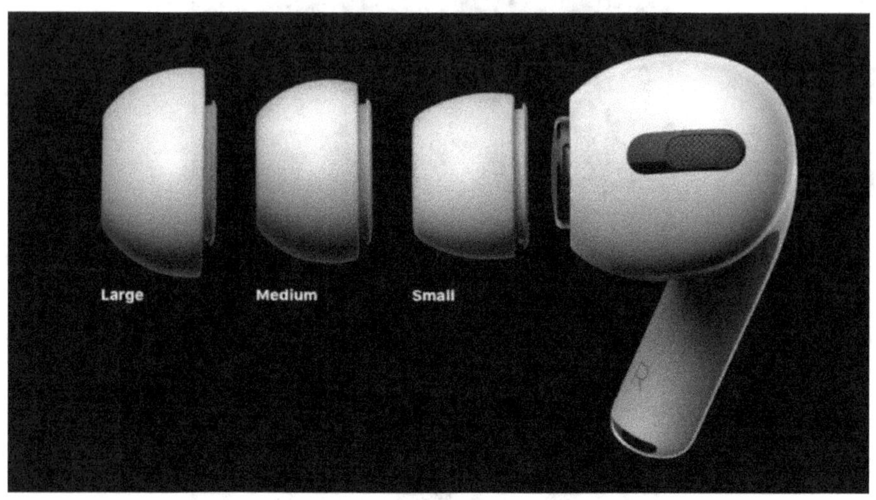

4. Line up the oval shape of the new ear tips and press into place (you'll hear a click).

How to Have AirPods Pro Announce Your Calls

To find out who's calling, normally you'd have to take out your iPhone or look at your Apple Watch, but you can have your AirPods Pro announce who it is, saving you the trouble. To enable this feature, simply follow these steps.

1. On your iPhone, go to **Settings**.
2. Select **Phone** in the list.
3. Select **Announce Calls**.
4. Select **Headphones Only** to tick the checkbox.

With this, the iPhone will announce who's calling you only if a call is received when wearing AirPods Pro earbuds.

How to Get Siri to Read Your Messages without Unlocking Your iPhone

To set this up, make sure your iPhone or iPad is running iOS 13.2 or iPadOS 13.2 respectively. Turning the **Announce Messages** feature on is easy, once you are on the right iOS or iPadOS. To turn on Announce Messages:

1. Open **Settings** on your iPhone or iPad.

2. Tap on **Notifications**.

3. Scroll down to **Announce Messages with Siri**.

4. Toggle Annonce Messages with Siri **On**

5. In the Announce Messages From section, tap on **Messages**.

6. Toggle **On** Announce Messages with Siri at the top

7. Choose from **Favorites, Recents, Contacts** and **Everyone**.

How to Reply to Messages with Siri

Siri will listen after reading out your message to allow you to reply without having to say **Hey Siri** first. This means that you can just say **Reply**, followed by a dictation of your reply. To do this, follow these steps.

1. Wait for Siri to read the message. Siri then listens for your reply.

2. Tell Siri you'd like to reply, and then speak your message. Say something like **Reply I'm on my way** or **Tell her I'll meet you there**.

3. When you stop talking, Siri reads your reply back to you and asks if you want to send it.

You can also have Siri send your reply immediately, without reading it back first.

1. Go to **Settings** and tap **Notifications**.

2. Select **Announce Messages with Siri**.

3.   Scroll down to **Reply Without Confirmation.**

4.   Toggle Reply Without Confirmation **On**

How to Use AirPods Pro's Live Listen Feature to Spy on Others

AirPods Pro comes with the **Live Listen** feature, which allows an iPhone or iPad to serve as a remote microphone. It turns your iPhone's microphone into the listening device and your AirPods Pro into a speaker. After you turn this feature on, you can put your iPhone in the next room (upside down so as to not give it away), and go to the next room and listen to everything. As long as you're in about 30 feet range of AirPods Pro, you can hear everything from that next room.

To add **Live Listen** to Control Centre, follow the steps below:

1.   Open the **Settings** menu and go to **Control Center**.

2.   Tap **Customize Controls**.

3.   Scroll down and tap **circled +** icon next to **Hearing** icon.

4.   Tap **Back** to save and exit the Control Center settings.

To access and use **Live Listen** feature after adding it to the Control Center, follow the steps below.

1.   Open **Control Center**.

2.   Tap **Hearing** icon (the icon with an image of an ear) while your AirPods Pro is connected to your iPhone.

3. Tap **Live Listen** to instantly start hearing through your iPhone microphone.

How to Share Audio with Two Different Pairs of AirPods Pro

Apple's iOS 13 and iPadOS 13 come with a new Audio Sharing feature that lets you listen the same audio with a friend on two different pairs of AirPods Pro without disturbing those around you. To do this, follow these steps.

1. With your AirPods Pro on, start playing audio on your iPhone or iPad.
2. Open Control Centre and go to the **Now Playing** section.
3. Tap **AirPlay** icon.
4. Bring your friend's AirPods Pro inside their case close to your iPhone or iPad and flip the lid open.
5. You should see a prompt on your device's screen offering to **Share Audio** with the second pair of AirPods Pro.
6. Select **Share Audio** and then ask your friend to tap **Join** on his/her device.

How to Find Your Misplaced or Lost AirPods Pro

If you lose or misplace your AirPods Pro, you can find their last known location in the **Find My** app.

1. Open **Find My** app on your iOS device (or access it in any browser via **iCloud.com**).
2. Tap the **Devices** tab at the bottom of the screen.
3. Tap your Airpods Pro in the list.

4. Tap **Play Sound** if you're fairly sure your AirPods Pro earbud(s) are somewhere within earshot. If you don't know where you lost your earbud(s), the last place they were connected will be shown on the map — tap **Directions** to get directions to the last known location.

How to Check Your AirPods Pro's Firmware Version and Serial Number

To check the version of the firmware that you have installed to make sure it's up to date, follow these steps:

1. Go to **Settings** on your iOS device
2. Tap **General**
3. Tap **About**
4. Tap **AirPods Pro**
5. Check the numbers shown beside **Firmware Version** and **Serial Number** entries.

How to Update Your AirPods Pro's Firmware

Apple occasionally releases firmware updates for its AirPods Pro earbuds that can include performance improvements, feature tweaks and bug fixes. If you want to make sure your AirPods Pro are up to date with the latest firmware, and then follow the steps below.

1. Insert your AirPods Pro in their case if they aren't already.
2. Connect the AirPods Pro charging case to a power source using the included Lightning to USB cable, or alternatively on a wireless charging case.

3.   Move the iPhone or iPad that the AirPods Pro has been paired with near to the charging case, and make sure the iOS device has an internet connection.

And that's all there is to it. After a short while, any available software updates should be automatically downloaded and installed. If you're having trouble updating your AirPods Pro, make sure the charging case is fully charged. You can also try resetting the AirPods Pro.

How to Reset AirPods Pro

If your AirPods Pro aren't working as they should be – if you can't connect to them or if they won't charge, for example – you can reset them by following these steps.

1.   Place your AirPods Pro earbuds in the charging case and close the lid

2.   Wait 30 seconds, then open the lid.

3.   On your iOS or iPadOS device, go to **Settings** and tap **Bluetooth**.

4.   Tap the **circled i** next to your AirPods Pro.

5.   Tap **Forget This Device**, and tap again to confirm

6.   With the AirPods Pro case lid open, press and hold the button on the back of the case for about 15 seconds until you see the status light flashing amber.

7.   With the case lid open, place your AirPods Pro close to your device and follow the steps on your device's screen to reconnect your AirPods Pro.

Note that now the AirPods Pro is reset; they will no longer automatically recognize any of the devices linked to your iCloud account. Opening the AirPods Pro case near to an iOS device will initiate the setup process, just like the first time.